Investing for Kids Age 13 and Above

Table of Contents

Disclaimer

Our Gift

As part of our gratitude for buying our book, we'd like to give you a special gift. It's a list of 100 investing principles that we summarized based on the investing habits and interviews of Warren Buffett, Michael Burry, Carl Icahn, Bill Gross and Charlie Munger. If you haven't heard of them, they're possibly five of the best investors of all time.

https://investing.grwebsite.com/

Bobby, who was an introverted teenager, continually felt a sense of trepidation whenever people around him started talking about money. He witnessed a lot of stress and turmoil through tough monetary times that his parents faced in 2008. He yearned for a stronger future but was usually left dazed and stressed when he tried to understand the basics of finance and investing.

One day, while snooping through a bookshelf in his best friends' room, he came across the book "Investing for Kids Age 13 and Above". He checked out the first few pages of the book and it seemed easy to read, and also had a lot of useful information. He right away went home and bought the book on Amazon.

Bobby read the book and started doing the exercises and activities at the back of the book. He felt a sense of strong empowerment through being able to understand the financial basics. He no longer felt lost and overwhelmed when thinking about money. He instantly started to grow his savings. He gained confidence and began to dream of a brighter future. He finally got a sense of purpose and drive for his life.

A few years later, he had constructed a decent financial savings buffer. He browsed through his bookshelf, searching for the book again. He skipped to the chapter on investments. The stock market chapter was at the start intimidating for Bobby, but he persevered. Through the book's guidance, he gained a deep understanding of an investment's risk and return, getting to know how to evaluate unique investment opportunities with confidence. The once-daunting financial markets became an opportunity for Bobby to enhance his wealth. He bought a few stocks, bonds and constructed a solid portfolio for the long term.

Bobby's lengthy emotional trip shows that knowledge is the best catalyst for change. The right attitude combined with a little information can take most people a long way forward. They can fight their circumstances and turn desires into reality. This book is a transformative ride that empowers young people like Bobby to rewire their economic hardwiring to gain a subsequent degree of economic success.

We're going to start off with the basics. Have you ever switched on CNBC and have no clue what they're talking about? Those words seem too complicated? What's a "dividend"? What's a "currency"?

We're going to familiarize you with some basic investing terms. You're not going to be an expert after reading this chapter. But you're going to start building a foundation of knowledge, on top of which you will improve over time.

In this first section, you're going to find these common simple financial terms in the word search puzzle below. The answers for all puzzles are at the back of the book.

```
D  N  E  G  Q  G  Y  Z  H  S  B  L  P  K  U
X  U  M  V  U  M  T  Y  N  K  O  V  L  Q  W
I  H  O  E  V  U  F  H  A  O  D  J  V  C  Z
N  L  V  J  T  S  E  V  N  I  H  N  J  R  D
V  U  R  D  Y  S  A  V  I  N  G  S  B  Z  L
I  I  D  E  A  M  J  X  F  Q  H  I  Z  Z  V
K  F  N  E  R  P  R  O  F  I  T  G  E  A  A
W  O  U  G  X  X  B  P  Z  N  J  V  O  S  G
M  I  F  E  Y  V  S  Q  V  E  Y  Y  M  E  F
B  Q  J  Z  P  F  T  A  E  E  U  X  Q  J  Z
U  T  I  Y  L  M  K  N  A  B  R  I  K  O  O
H  F  Q  L  Z  L  M  M  W  A  E  A  E  F  K
N  H  S  H  R  X  E  V  D  G  R  J  H  S  E
R  M  A  S  L  P  W  S  I  D  T  Y  R  S  U
D  D  C  U  R  R  E  N  C  Y  F  S  S  R  M
```

MONEY	CURRENCY	SAVINGS
BUY	SELL	SHARE
BANK	INVEST	PROFIT

```
N  V  G  U  Z  H  T  W  O  R  G  G  P  A  K
I  E  N  Y  E  F  J  L  U  C  P  X  B  K  U
A  N  C  I  N  J  Q  W  C  X  A  S  D  P  E
L  H  T  N  W  A  A  P  E  T  O  S  T  I  F
V  K  A  E  A  K  P  Y  E  N  Q  M  E  U  D
T  D  E  Z  R  W  H  M  X  U  J  Q  G  Y  C
G  S  I  B  U  E  O  W  O  O  K  G  D  X  A
O  N  Q  V  U  N  S  L  O  C  M  R  U  H  E
X  Q  O  X  I  T  H  T  L  C  B  B  B  S  N
B  T  V  G  O  D  S  E  U  A  G  S  Y  X  X
M  F  L  C  V  F  E  F  I  K  M  W  K  G  Q
B  O  K  A  X  Q  T  N  R  N  S  L  B  F  T
U  C  L  B  H  E  L  F  D  A  W  I  O  A  S
N  U  V  S  I  X  Y  I  A  B  Y  Y  R  L  U
E  Y  F  U  Q  A  V  M  J  I  O  B  S  H  L
```

RISK	STOCK	COMPANY
GROWTH	VALUE	DIVIDEND
BANKACCOUNT	BUDGET	INTEREST
ALLOWANCE		

Challenge #3

```
W  I  A  Y  G  E  C  I  D  S  H  C  C  U  V  L  M  A  A  B
I  G  M  T  R  Q  W  O  S  P  V  R  X  A  E  T  R  A  M  L
J  G  R  W  M  A  I  E  B  G  L  X  E  X  P  E  N  S  E  E
T  P  R  U  E  N  E  R  P  E  R  T  N  E  S  G  E  X  M  X
D  X  O  D  T  F  B  I  V  P  L  R  K  K  N  D  R  L  O  O
N  T  Y  N  V  A  D  U  F  P  I  P  Q  E  G  U  P  W  C  O
I  W  V  U  Z  T  E  K  R  A  M  K  D  C  B  B  O  A  N  M
S  J  P  J  J  E  O  J  C  G  B  I  N  G  S  Z  X  M  I  J
N  M  Y  Q  X  R  Q  G  M  Z  N  S  S  W  T  W  Y  E  V  L
U  J  R  W  L  Z  V  D  I  F  L  I  B  S  P  I  I  F  U  R
P  K  S  F  G  E  H  E  L  D  Z  B  T  W  Y  J  O  G  K  S
Q  N  B  Y  T  I  R  A  H  C  A  A  J  E  U  T  A  Q  D  G
L  U  A  M  D  H  T  W  G  Q  O  J  I  J  G  N  N  T  H  R
H  M  P  S  M  I  F  I  N  A  N  C  E  D  W  D  S  P  A  D
Q  Z  D  S  O  A  E  C  K  M  Z  Q  L  Y  Y  A  U  Z  P  L
Y  C  Z  N  X  A  M  B  P  P  B  B  T  Z  X  G  Z  B  D  A
I  N  K  P  T  I  X  D  X  R  S  B  H  L  X  X  U  L  K  V
W  D  I  V  H  K  G  I  H  Z  Z  E  B  E  N  Y  Y  G  Z  S
G  U  S  I  I  D  B  T  W  R  I  X  D  R  J  I  L  D  C  N
C  V  S  H  S  R  A  X  X  B  K  V  P  M  R  E  H  U  H  T
```

INFLATION	MARKET	ENTREPRENEUR
EXPENSE	BUDGET	CHARITY
INCOME	FINANCE	BUDGETING

```
O  K  A  I  H  D  S  I  Q  Z  A  R  I  M  O
Y  E  M  L  Q  G  D  R  R  M  L  V  N  W  Y
D  N  O  B  P  I  Y  I  I  B  Q  N  V  H  V
N  D  R  P  B  H  B  X  N  J  A  I  E  D  T
N  U  K  V  S  N  S  C  S  T  E  J  S  M  O
H  I  Q  V  W  M  X  D  W  V  E  P  T  V  C
N  V  B  V  O  X  M  N  N  J  G  R  M  F  G
Z  W  N  Y  N  L  F  U  C  H  G  W  E  A  I
Y  U  O  U  U  V  S  F  P  O  W  Y  N  S  K
N  Z  B  T  Q  U  U  L  I  M  F  S  T  E  T
O  D  C  C  P  P  M  A  L  D  S  Y  W  B  M
K  I  N  D  E  X  F  U  N  D  T  B  E  D  M
K  J  X  G  R  Q  J  T  X  M  O  P  G  A  G
D  O  X  O  O  R  X  U  V  V  C  N  I  I  N
T  X  S  H  A  J  F  M  R  U  K  K  A  M  W
```

DEBT	INTEREST	INVESTMENT
STOCK	MUTUALFUND	INDEXFUND
BOND	IRA	

Now, let's have a look at what these terms mean. Read through these to familiarize yourself with what each term and section means. You're going to need these in the next set of challenges.

1. **Money:** A medium that stores value and facilitates exchange between two parties.

2. **Currency:** A form of money which consists of physical coins and banknotes.

3. **Saving:** Amount of money left over after spending.

4. **Buy:** Purchase by giving money for an item

5. **Sell:** Give an item away in exchange for money

6. **Share:** Smallest possible unit of ownership in a company.

7. **Bank:** A financial entity that allows one to store, save, borrow or loan money.

8. **Invest:** Allocate money in a certain manner to obtain profit or income.

9. **Profit:** Financial gain from a business activity after subtracting all expenses.

10. **Risk:** Probability of loss from performing an activity.

11. **Company:** A legal entity formed by a single person or group of persons for the purpose of conducting business.

12. **Growth:** Increase in value of a company or business' financial performance over time.

13. **Value:** The worth or importance assigned to something. In finance, it's the worth assigned to a company.

14. **Dividend:** A payment made by a company to its shareholders as a reward for holding its stock

15. **Savings account:** A bank account where people can save money and earn interest over the long term.

16. **Allowance:** A fixed monthly amount given to a person by a guardian or parent.

17. **Financial goal:** A fixed goal that is related to savings or investment for eg. saving a fixed amount for retirement.

18. **Entrepreneur:** A person who starts a business.

19. **Market:** A physical or virtual place where a group of buyers and sellers meet to exchange goods and/or services.

20. **Budgeting:** The act of creating a budget.

21. **Charity:** The act of giving money, items or services to people in need of it.

22. **Income:** Money that is earnt by a person through work or dividend.

23. **Expense:** Money that is spent on a certain item.

24. **Savings:** Money that you set aside for future use, such as a rainy day or a big purchase.

25. **Budget:** A plan for how a person, company or Government can spend and save their income.

26. **Debt:** The total amount owed to someone after you lend it to someone.

27. **Interest:** The cost per year to borrow money.

28. **Investment:** A way to allocate money in the hope of profit and income.

29. **Stock:** A unit of ownership in a company. It's the same as a share.

30. **Mutual fund:** A company that takes in money from investors and allocates it to different companies.

31. **Bond:** An investment where you loan money to a government, government agency or company.

32. **IRA:** A savings account used to save money for one's retirement.

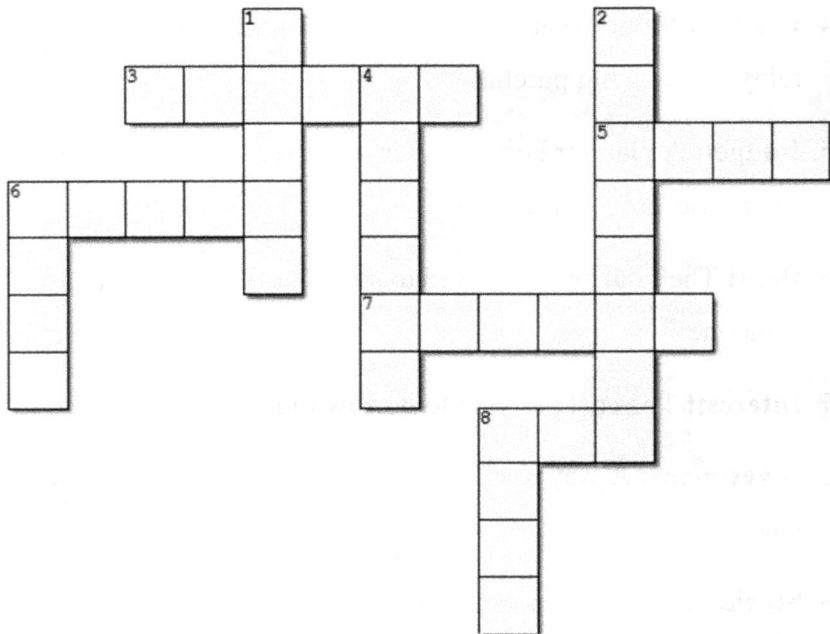

Across

3. Financial gain from a business activity after subtracting all expenses.
5. Probability of loss from performing an activity.
6. Smallest possible unit of ownership in a company.
7. Amount of money left over after spending.
8. Purchase by giving money for an item

Down

1. A medium that stores value and facilities exchange between two parties.
2. A form of money which consists of physical coins and banknotes.
4. Allocate money in a certain manner to obtain profit or income.
6. Give an item away in exchange for money
8. A financial entity that allows one to store, save, borrow or loan money.

Challenge #6

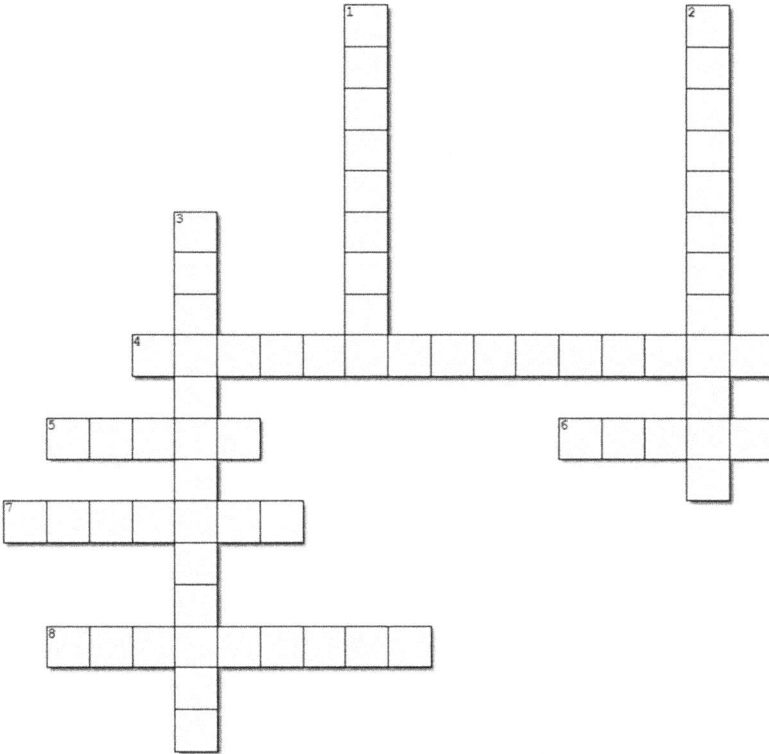

Across

4. A Bank account where people can earn interest and save money over the long term
5. Same as a share of a company
6. The worth or importance assigned to something
7. A legal entity that is formed by a single person or group for the purpose of conducting business
8. A fixed monthly amount given to a person by a parent or guardian

Down

1. The act of creating a budget
2. A person who starts a business
3. A fixed goal that is related to savings or investment

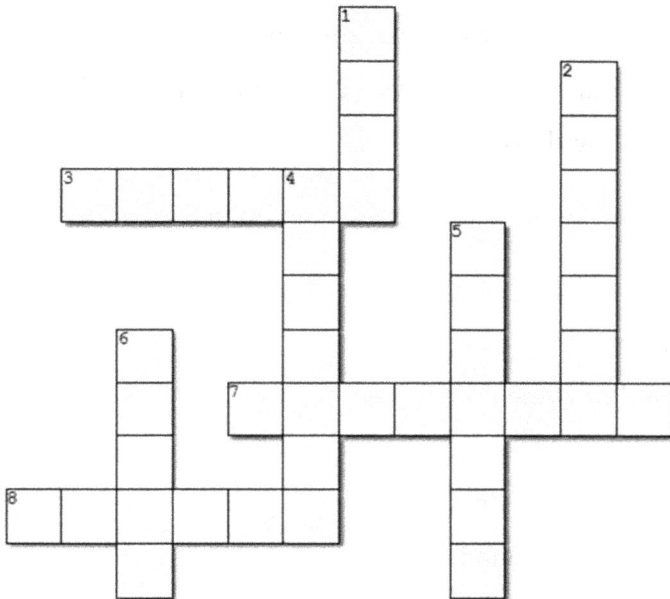

Across

3. A plan for how a person, company or Government can spend and save their income.

7. The cost per year to borrow money.

8. Money that is earnt by a person through work or dividend.

Down

1. The total amount owed to someone after you lend it to someone.

2. Money that you set aside for future use, such as a rainy day or a big purchase.

4. Money that is spent on a certain item.

5. The act of giving money, items or services to people in need of it.

6. A share of ownership in a company.

Fun Money-Making Activities for Kids

So, what's a great way to make some pocket money so you can get started on your financial journey? You got to first make money before you can save and invest.

Here's a few simple activities you can do to earn a little extra pocket money.

1. Babysitting
2. Walking dogs
3. Feeding Pets
4. Selling stuff online
5. Lemonade stand
6. Selling water in the park
7. Tutoring Math
8. Tutoring English
9. Online Tutoring
10. Social media Influencer
11. Youtuber
12. Car Washing
13. House Sitting
14. Blogging
15. Video Blogging

16. Data Entry
17. Bake sale
18. Popcorn sale
19. Gardening
20. Paint fences
21. Flea Market
22. Clean boats
23. Selling stuff on Amazon
24. Selling on Etsy
25. Fold Laundry
26. Ghost-writing
27. Virtual Assistant
28. Graphic Design

Challenge #8

Write down 5 activities that you like the most below:

Write down 5 actions that you will take this week to start working on these activities:

"Living life without a goal is like sailing a boat without a destination"

– Fitzhugh Dodson

The strongest boat will eventually run out of fuel and sink in a snowstorm. People have mixed feelings about setting financial goals. Some see them as boring and unnecessary, while others are really excited about the process of sailing towards their financial future.

Financial goals are extremely important for every single person. It is difficult to save money without being motivated by a goal. Life would seem bland if one was just saving money without any idea where to put it to use. Once you visualize the house, or the lifestyle you want, the business, the sailboat can see the land that you are looking for.

For the purposes of this book, we are going to look at the basics of setting financial targets and look at simple examples that everyone can use.

Financial Goal

The first thing to do is to set your financial goal with a good level of detail. Write out your financial goal below with the actual amount, and the time within which you need to achieve your financial goal. You might need to spend some time to research the cost of the item if you haven't already done so.

What is your Financial Goal? _____

What are you saving for? _____

How much time do you need to save?_____

What is the exact amount?_____

Visualize Your Financial Goal

In one sentence, write out why you need to achieve your financial goal. Is it an impulsive purchase? Do you want to buy it for your mom? Or do you want to show off to your friends?

Think about how happy you would be if you reached your goal. Picture yourself in your mind. Then, draw a picture of yourself after you have achieved your financial goal. If it's an item you're saving for, you can draw the item below. You can also print out a picture of yourself with the item and paste it below.

How Much Have You Saved Up?

The first thing to do after setting your financial goal is to have a look at how ready you are to achieve your financial goal.

How much money have you saved for your goal? Remember, this is not your total savings. This is the just the amount you've set aside up for your goal.

Then, you're going to calculate your monthly income. This is just your annual salary divided by 12. For your monthly expenses, you can look at your credit card statement and calculate your total last 12 months, and then divide by 12. This will tell you your total monthly savings.

Divided the total amount you need over your total monthly savings. This will tell you how many months to achieving your goal.

Fill out the form below to make the calculation easier.

Current Financial Position

Total Money Saved for Goal:_____

Monthly Income:_____

Monthly Expenses:_____

Saving Per Month:_____(Monthly Income – Monthly Expenses)

Months to Goal:_____(Goal Savings / Savings Per Month)

Monthly Income Breakdown

Well, now let's break down your monthly income. Most of you will just have one income source. You can list that down below with the amount. If you have additional income, you can list that here.

Monthly Income Breakdown

Income Source 1 (_____) = _____

Income Source 2 (_____) = _____

Income Source 3 (_____) = _____

Income Source 4 (_____) = _____

Monthly Expenses Breakdown:

You can do the same for your expenses. Write down all the costs for health, food, housing, transportation etc. below. This can come from your credit card or banking statement.

Monthly Expenses Breakdown

Housing Cost = _____

Food Cost = _____

Transportation Cost = _____

Entertainment Cost = _____

Health Costs = _____

Others = _____

Monthly Subscriptions:

Now, let's list out all those subscriptions you have. It's important to have an idea of what fixed costs are coming out of your bank account or credit card. Make sure you list the most expensive subscriptions first, as these have the biggest impact on your wallet.

Monthly Expense Subscriptions
(most expensive to least)

Subscription Service 1 = _____

Subscription Service 2 = _____

Subscription Service 3 = _____

Subscription Service 4 = _____

Subscription Service 5 = _____

Subscription Service 6 = _____

Other Subscriptions = _____

Now, what happens if you want to change your goal? You want to achieve it faster? Then fill out the form below which calculates exactly how much extra you need to save each month to achieve the new goal.

In the form below, you basically calculate the monthly savings needed to achieve the new time goal. Then, you subtract the current monthly savings from it to calculate how much extra you need per month.

SUPERCHARGE GOAL

New time goal= _____

Monthly Savings Needed = Savings Goal / New time goal = _____

Extra Monthly Savings Needed = Monthly Savings Needed - Current Monthly Savings = _____

Armed with the knowledge of exactly how much you need to save, you can now look at the options you can use to do so. You can either get an extra job, extra income source, work extra hours at your job. Or you can cut expenses. You can reduce some of your subscriptions and other expenses. Fill out the form below to help you plan your new goal.

An Example - Sam and his Car

Now, let's have a look at an example. Sam is looking to save money for a car. He's looking to buy a used Toyota Corolla for $10000. Now, Sam fills out his Financial Goals chart to figure out where he stands.

What is your Financial Goal? _To save money for a car_

What are you saving for? ___To buy a used Toyota Corolla_

How much time do you need to save?___1-2 years_

What is the exact amount?___$10000_

Why do I need this? _So I can go out with friends on a regular basis_

Draw a picture of yourself after having achieved this goal below

He needs to save $10000 in around 1-2 years to buy a used Toyota Corolla. He's visualized his goal and the reason for the goal, so he remains motivated over time.

Total Money Saved for Goal:__$0_____

Monthly Income:_$2000_____

Monthly Expenses:__$1500_____

Saving Per Month:_$2000-$1500=$500_____(Monthly Income – Monthly Expenses)

Months to Goal:_$10000/$500 = 20 months_____(Goal Savings / Savings Per Month)

Sam has not yet started saving for his goal. He has a monthly income (after tax) of $2000 with expenses of $1500. So, he saves around $500 per month. With his current income and expenses, he can achieve his goal within 20 months. This is within his goal of 1-2 years.

Now, let's have a look at Sam's income and expenses. He has 1 job of working part time at a café that provides all his income. When he breaks down his expenses, he notices that housing, food and transportation make up most of his costs. The rest is just $500 a month.

He has 4 monthly subscriptions for his health insurance, Netflix, Hulu and Amazon Prime.

Monthly Income Breakdown

Income Source 1 (Café job) = **$2000**

Income Source 2 (_____) = _____

Income Source 3 (_____) = _____

Income Source 4 (_____) = _____

Monthly Expenses Breakdown

Housing Cost = **$500**

Food Cost = **$200**

Transportation Cost = **$300**

Entertainment Cost = **$200**

Health Costs = **$50**

Others = **$250**

Monthly Expense Subscriptions
(most expensive to least)

Subscription Service 1 = _$50 (Health Insurance)_____

Subscription Service 2 = ___$20 (Netflix)_____

Subscription Service 3 = _$15 (Hulu)_____

Subscription Service 4 = _$10 (Amazon Prime)_____

Subscription Service 5 = _____

Subscription Service 6 = _____

Other Subscriptions = _____

Now, Sam realizes that he'd like to complete his goal within 1 year. He doesn't want to wait 20 months. He needs it in 12 months.

So, Sam needs an extra $333 per month to reach his savings goal in 12 months. Sam has to either an earn $333 extra per month or save that amount; or a combination of both.

So, let's have a look at what Sam can do below.

OPTIONS TO SUPERCHARGE GOAL

Extra Job: _____

Extra hours at job: _____

Extra Income Source: _____

Subscription to cut: _____

Other Costs to cut: _____

OPTIONS TO SUPERCHARGE GOAL

Extra Job: _____

Extra hours at job: **25 hrs = $250 per month**

Extra Income Source: _____

Subscription to cut: _____

Other Costs to cut: **$100 per month on entertainment**

Increased savings: **$100 + $250 =** _____

Sam thinks about whether he should get a second job. He decides that he likes the job that he works at, and he's going to work 25 hours extra per month. At a wage of $10 per hour, he's going to get an extra $250 per month closer to his goal.

Sam went through his subscriptions and his other expenses. He decides that he doesn't have any high-cost subscriptions that he wants to cut. He decides to cut down on monthly entertainment by $100 for 1 year.

Sam saves an extra $350 per month with his new plan and will be able to buy his car after 1 year.

Now, it's time to set your financial goal. List out your goal and the reason for your financial goal.

What is your Financial Goal? _____

What are you saving for? _____

How much time do you need to save?_____

What is the exact amount?_____

Why do I need this? _____

Draw a picture of yourself after having achieved this goal below

List out your income, expenses and determine how long it will take you reach your goal.

Current Financial Position

Total Money Saved for Goal:_____

Monthly Income:_____

Monthly Expenses:_____

Saving Per Month:_____(Monthly Income – Monthly Expenses)

Months to Goal:_____(Goal Savings / Savings Per Month)

Monthly Income Breakdown

Income Source 1 (_____) = _____

Income Source 2 (_____) = _____

Income Source 3 (_____) = _____

Income Source 4 (_____) = _____

Monthly Expenses Breakdown

Housing Cost = _____

Food Cost = _____

Transportation Cost = _____

Entertainment Cost = _____

Health Costs = _____

Others = _____

Monthly Expense Subscriptions
(most expensive to least)

Subscription Service 1 = _____

Subscription Service 2 = _____

Subscription Service 3 = _____

Subscription Service 4 = _____

Subscription Service 5 = _____

Subscription Service 6 = _____

Other Subscriptions = _____

Challenge #12

Now, figure out how much extra you need to save to achieve the goal 1 year earlier.

SUPERCHARGE GOAL

New time goal= _____

Monthly Savings Needed = Savings Goal / New time goal = _____

Extra Monthly Savings Needed = Monthly Savings Needed - Current Monthly Savings = _____

OPTIONS TO SUPERCHARGE GOAL

Extra Job: _____

Extra hours at job: _____

Extra Income Source: _____

Subscription to cut: _____

Other Costs to cut: _____

Increased savings: _____

Savings Magic: Importance of Savings and Interest Rate

"A penny saved is a penny earned" according to Benjamin Franklin, one of the greatest innovators in American history. In the modern world of consumerism, one way to get ahead is to just get into the habit of saving money. Remember, it doesn't mean you stop spending. You just save a portion of what you earn. So, why exactly should you do it?

1. **Financial Stability:** Having a certain amount of savings provides you with a peace of mind financially. You're not worried that you'll be on the streets if you lose your job. It gives you a sense of control over your life and reduces your reliance on credit.

2. **Achieving Financial Goals:** The habit of planning and savings will help you achieve the financial goals you made for yourself in the previous chapter.

3. **Emergency Funds:** Now what happens if you or one of your family members is in an accident and needs expensive healthcare? What if your car breaks down? What if you lose your job? Your savings is your first line of defence against any calamity that might happen. We recommend an emergency savings buffer which allows you to live for 3-6 months without any income.

Interest Rates

If you invest your money in a bank or a bond, the interest rate is the percentage of your money that your bank pays you to hold the money. Think of it as loaning money to a bank at a fixed rate.

So, if you put $100 in a bank at 6% interest rate per year, you get paid 6% per year, or $6 per year.

But, here's one thing that's missing. You have $106 at the end of the 1st year ($100 + $6 interest). So, the interest on the 2nd year is calculated as 6% of $106. So, you get $6.36 interest for your second year; and you have $112.36 at the end of 2 years. This is called compound interest. The interest every year keeps increasing or compounding. Albert Einstein called compound interest the 8th wonder of the world. Here's a chart of how $100 grows over 15 years at a compound interest of 6%.

Amount In Bank

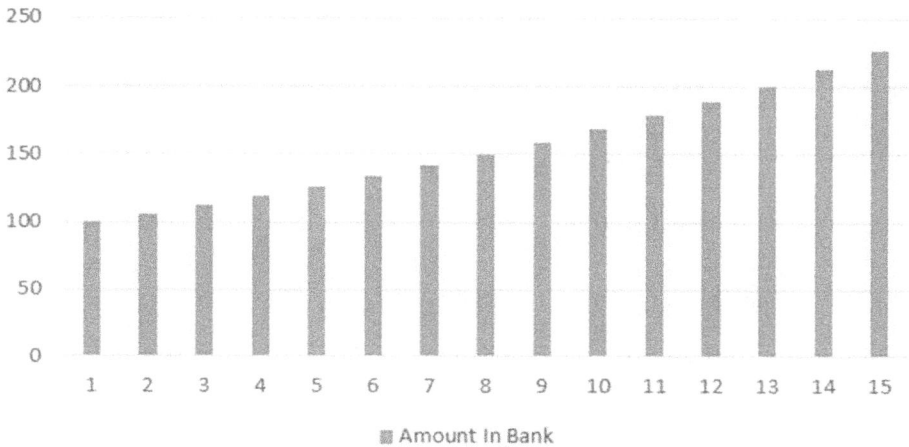

So, saving money in a bank with compounding interest rate can be a good way to increase your wealth over time.

Formula for Compound Interest:

The fastest way to calculate how compound interest is to use the below formula, where P is the initial amount, i is the interest rate and t is the time (or number of periods it has compounded).

$$A = P\left(1 + \frac{i}{100}\right)^t$$

So, for the above example:

$$A = 100\left(1 + \frac{6}{100}\right)^{15} = \$239.66$$

So, your $100 becomes $239.66 after 15 years of compounding at 6%. That's the beauty of saving money.

Challenge 13

You have a $1000 in the bank which has a compound interest of 7%. How much will that amount grow to in 10 years? Work it out below.

Andy has $1000 extra every year after subtracting all expenses from his income. How much does he have at the end of 4 years if he puts all his money in a savings account that pays 5% compound interest?

Fill out the table below to solve this problem.

	Amount Added	Interest	Total after interest + savings
End of Year 1	$1000		$1000
End of Year 2	$1000	$1000*1.05=$1050	$2050
End of Year 3	$1000	$2050*1.05=_____	_____
End of Year 4	$1000	_____	_____

"Inflation is as violent as a mugger, as frightening as an armed robber and as deadly as a hit man." This quote, by the late American President Ronald Reagan is as true today as it was during his time.

So, what exactly is inflation? Inflation is the rate of increase in prices of things we pay for. Inflation makes life more expensive, as it costs more to live the same way. Inflation is the reason rent goes up. It's the reason an apple costs more today than it did 5 years ago.

Here's a few examples of inflation below in the United States.

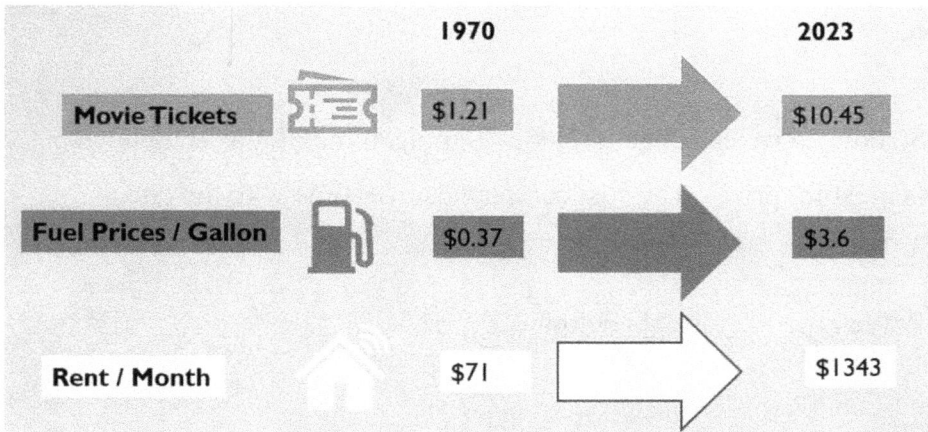

		1970		2023
Movie Tickets		$1.21	→	$10.45
Fuel Prices / Gallon		$0.37	→	$3.6
Rent / Month		$71	→	$1343

Why does Inflation Happen?

Inflation generally happens due to 3 reasons, with an additional 4th reason that causes temporary fluctuations in prices.

1. Increase in population leads to an increase in demands for goods and services, and prices go up.
2. Governments print more money which reaches the general population and more money to spend on the same number of goods and services.
3. Increase in debt allows customers to access more money to spend on goods and services.
4. Supply shocks such as floods, pandemics, droughts can cause a temporary decrease in supply of goods. This generally causes a temporary spike in prices.

So how do we calculate inflation? Simple, think of it as compound interest for prices. The cost compounds over time with the rate of inflation.

We can use the formula below:

$$NP = OP\left(1 + \frac{i}{100}\right)^t$$

Where NP is the new price, OP is the old price, i is the rate of inflation and t is the time period.

So, let's say 1 kg of apples cost $2 in 2010. What's the cost in 2025 given the rate of inflation is 4%?

Using the formula, we get the new price of 1 kg of apples NP as:

$$NP = 2\left(1 + \frac{4}{100}\right)^{15} = \$3.6$$

So, a kg of apples has changed in price from $2 to $3.60 due to inflation.

For example, if a gym membership costs $30 a month in 2020, what does it cost in 2030? Rate of inflation is 4%. Work it out below.

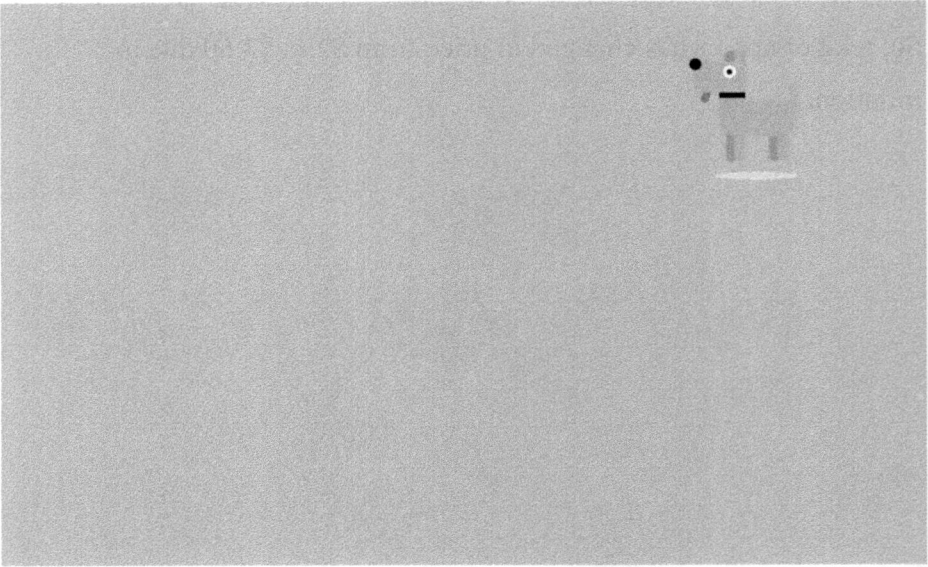

If an airline ticket costs $300 between Miami and Chicago in 2023, what will it cost in 2033? Rate of inflation is 5%. Work it out below.

Sam has $100 in the bank in 2020. Ally has $100 in the bank in 1970. Who is richer?

1970   **2020**

Ally has $100 in the bank   Sam has $100 in the bank

Who is richer? Sam or Ally?

Inflation is normal in every country. However, sometimes inflation gets out of control. Government prints too much money for the economy to absorb. Sometimes, the Government takes on too much foreign debt and is unable to repay. The currency crashes and becomes less valuable. Economy sometimes becomes too unproductive due to external shocks like wars, pandemics, drought etc.

This has happened several times in recent history.

- Germany (Weimar Republic) in 1923

- Zimbabwe in 2005

- Venezuela (2018-present)

Hyperinflation is when prices increase by 50% or more per month. This is far more than the 3-5% inflation we have discussed in the previous examples. Hyperinflation has never happened in US history, though it has come close twice.

If you want to learn more about hyperinflation examples, you can check out our book Starving Billionaires.

Link: https://www.amazon.com/dp/B0997RR9FG

Here's a chilling example of hyperinflation. Solve the below problem to understand how hyperinflation works.

You are living in Venezuela. A loaf of bread costs a 100 Bolivars in June. The rate of inflation is 100% per month. What is the cost of the loaf of bread in December?

Wandering Wallets: How Cost of Living Varies Everywhere

According to a Pew Research survey in 2018, 27% of Americans have never travelled outside the country. With America being a relatively wealthy country, it is safe to assume that even fewer people have travelled overseas in most other countries. So, there are lots of people around the world who are not able to see how cost of living changes in different countries, or within their own country. As of 2023, a 1-bedroom apartment in New York costs an average of $3769 while the same costs $1133 in Toledo, Ohio. Going further away, it costs $275 in Bangalore, India. You can do a similar comparison for food, transportation, entertainment costs. It's very important to understand this concept, as it could significantly impact your financial life. Here's why:

A. **Salary Negotiations:** If you get a job in another state or country, the ability to do a proper cost of living comparison will help you better negotiate a salary with your future employer.

B. **Relocation Decision:** If you're relocating to a new city, it will help you understand exactly how much you need to live in a new area.

C. **Financial Planning:** This will help you decide how much savings you need to move to a new city, and how far your salary (if you are location independent) will help you if you move.

Now Let's Compare

So, how do we do this? We use information from cost of living comparison tool Numbeo (www.numbeo.com). And there's two ways to go about this.

Method 1: Pancake Method

One way is to just do a general comparison between the two cities. Numbeo gives you a percentage difference between the two cities. Just simply multiply your monthly living expenses by the ratio. This method is called the Pancake method because it assumes the lifestyle all across the world is flat and the same, like a pancake.

So, let's look at an example. Bob is currently living in Chicago, USA. He is thinking about moving to Bangkok, Thailand. He plugs in the two cities in Numbeo and comes up with below screenshot. We can see that Bangalore is 45% cheaper than Chicago.

So, we need to multiply Bob's monthly Chicago expenses by 55% (100% - 45%) to get his expected monthly costs in Bangkok.

If Bob spends $3000 a month in Chicago, he would be expected to spend 55% of $3000; or **$1650** a month in Bangkok.

NUMBEO   Select City

Cost Of Living ▾   Property Prices ▾   Quality Of Life ▾   Premium ▾

Cost of Living › Compare Cities › United States vs Thailand › Chicago, IL vs Bangkok

Cost of Living Comparison Between Chicago, IL and Bangkok ⇆

You would need around 3,171.5$ (110,680.3฿) in Bangkok to maintain the same standard of life that you can have with 6,700.0$ in Chicago, IL (assuming you rent in both cities). This calculation uses our Cost of Living Plus Rent Index to compare the cost of living and assume net earnings (after income tax). You can change the amount in this calculation.

Indices Difference ⓘ

Consumer Prices in Bangkok are 45.1% lower than in Chicago, IL (without rent)
Consumer Prices Including Rent in Bangkok are 52.7% lower than in Chicago, IL
Rent Prices in Bangkok are 64.4% lower than in Chicago, IL
Restaurant Prices in Bangkok are 69.9% lower than in Chicago, IL
Groceries Prices in Bangkok are 44.8% lower than in Chicago, IL
Local Purchasing Power in Bangkok is 77.9% lower than in Chicago, IL

Currency: USD ▾   Sticky Currency   Switch to US measurement units

Method 2: Biriyani Method

This method is named after a popular Indian dish called the biriyani. Biriyani is a dish which tastes different in different parts of India and different parts of the world. It even tastes different based on who is cooking it, even after assuming the same ingredients.

So, this method assumes the same living expenses all over the world. It calculates the cost of each expense (or ingredient) and mixes them together to see what the total cost is.

So, let's say Bob breaks down his $3000 monthly spend into:

$1600 a month rent 1-bedroom apartment

$350 a month groceries

$500 a month eating at restaurants

$100 a month health insurance

$150 a month public transport

$300 a month utilities (internet, phone and heating)

Now, let's have a look at each of these using Numbeo's tool

1-Bedroom Apartment	$310.17
Groceries	20% less than $500 = **$400**
Restaurants	70% less than $500 = **$150**
Health Insurance	**$40** (International Travel Insurance)
Public Transport	**$75**
Internet	**$15.25**
Phone	**$14.13**
Heating / AC	**$82.71**
Other Expenses:	
Visa	$60/12 = **$5**
Round Trip Air Ticket once a year	$1200/12 = **$100**
Total	**$1192.26**

Fixed Costs:

Cost of housing, internet, phone, heating and AC can be taken directly from Numbeo's tool. Just copy and paste the expenses into the table. As an example, we can see the rent for a 1 bedroom in Bangkok is $310.17 outside the city center. So we paste that amount in the expenses table above.

	Chicago, IL	Bangkok	
1 Pair of Men Leather Business Shoes	(4,522.26 ฿)	(3,383.96 ฿)	-25.2 %
Rent Per Month	✏ Edit	✏ Edit	
Apartment (1 bedroom) in City Centre	2,068.65 $ (72,192.68 ฿)	720.74 $ (25,152.78 ฿)	-65.2 %
Apartment (1 bedroom) Outside of Centre	1,483.58 $ (51,774.57 ฿)	310.17 $ (10,824.32 ฿)	-79.1 %
Apartment (3 bedrooms) in City Centre	4,114.71 $ (143,597.06 ฿)	1,800.91 $ (62,848.94 ฿)	-56.2 %
Apartment (3 bedrooms) Outside of Centre	2,917.86 $ (101,828.84 ฿)	933.96 $ (32,593.75 ฿)	-68.0 %
Buy Apartment Price	Chicago, IL ✏ Edit	Bangkok ✏ Edit	
Price per Square Meter to Buy Apartment in City Centre	3,881.74 $ (135,466.74 ฿)	5,616.29 $ (196,000.00 ฿)	+44.7 %
Price per Square Meter to Buy Apartment Outside of Centre	2,727.31 $ (95,178.88 ฿)	2,585.26 $ (89,523.61 ฿)	-5.9 %
Salaries And Financing	Chicago, IL ✏ Edit	Bangkok ✏ Edit	
Average Monthly Net Salary (After Tax)	6,329.36 $ (220,865.01 ฿)	663.61 $ (23,159.01 ฿)	-89.5 %
Mortgage Interest Rate in Percentages (%), Yearly, for 20 Years Fixed-Rate	6.65	5.68	-14.6 %
Last update:	July 2023	July 2023	
Contributors in the past 12 months:	277	360	

Food:

Food is a little complicated since everyone spends money on different items. So, just have a look at the top items in the list below, and average out the cost difference as seen below:

Imported Beer (0.33 liter bottle)	(279.19 B)	(150.00 B)	
Cappuccino (regular)	5.23 $ (182.37 B)	2.29 $ (80.02 B)	-56.1 %
Coke/Pepsi (0.33 liter bottle)	2.64 $ (91.96 B)	0.60 $ (21.07 B)	-77.1 %
Water (0.33 liter bottle)	2.13 $ (74.44 B)	0.36 $ (12.39 B)	-83.4 %

🛒 Markets	Chicago, IL ✏ Edit	Bangkok ✏ Edit	
Milk (regular), (1 liter)	1.00 $ (35.01 B)	1.66 $ (57.96 B)	+65.8
Loaf of Fresh White Bread (500g)	3.72 $ (129.69 B)	1.68 $ (58.79 B)	-54.7 %
Rice (white), (1kg)	5.02 $ (175.18 B)	1.51 $ (52.76 B)	-89.9 %
Eggs (regular) (12)	4.50 $ (157.04 B)	2.06 $ (71.94 B)	-54.2 %
Local Cheese (1kg)	15.81 $ (551.87 B)	18.01 $ (628.64 B)	13.9 %
Chicken Fillets (1kg)	12.07 $ (421.38 B)	3.32 $ (115.82 B)	-72.
Beef Round (1kg) (or Equivalent Back Leg Red Meat)	17.69 $ (617.38 B)	11.49 $ (400.83 B)	-35.1 %
Apples (1kg)	5.44 $ (189.88 B)	2.93 $ (102.10 B)	-46.2 %
Banana (1kg)	1.76 $ (61.55 B)	1.34 $ (46.71 B)	-24.1 %

We see that the top 5 items are roughly 20% lower in Bangkok, Thailand. So, we take 80% of Chicago's grocery expense (80% of $500 = $400) as our expected expense in Bangkok.

We can do the same for restaurants below. We see that restaurants are roughly about 80% cheaper than Chicago. So, we take 20% of Chicago's restaurant expense as Bangkok's expected restaurant expense.

🍴 Restaurants	Chicago, IL ✏ Edit	Bangkok ✏ Edit	Difference
Meal, Inexpensive Restaurant	20.00 $ (697.97 B)	2.87 $ (100.00 B)	-85.7 %
Meal for 2 People, Mid-range Restaurant, Three-course	80.00 $ (2,791.88 B)	28.65 $ (1,000.00 B)	-64.2 %
McMeal at McDonalds (or Equivalent Combo Meal)	10.00 $	5.73 $	-42.7 %

Extra Costs:

Bob also wants to go back home once a year to see his family. So, he's included the cost of a round trip ticket to Chicago as an extra expense.

65

We need to divide that expense by 12 to get the expected monthly expense from the trip.

Everyone's going to have their own associated extra costs.

Total:

Bob's total in Bangkok is expected to be $1192.26. This is lower than the costs calculated using the Pancake method but not too far off. Keep in mind that these numbers are still an estimate but should give you a rough idea of what to expect in terms of costs.

Mary lives in San Francisco, California and wants to move to Miami, Florida. She spends $6000 a month in California. Use the pancake method to figure out how much she would be expected to spend in Miami if she moves there. Show your calculations below.

Simon lives in London, UK and wants to move to Bangalore, India. He spends a total of 1800 pounds a month in London. How much would he be expected to spend in Bangalore, India? Given he spends 800 pounds per month on rent, 300 pounds on utilities (phone, internet, electricity), 200 pounds on groceries and 500 pounds on restaurants.

Use both the pancake method and the biriyani method.

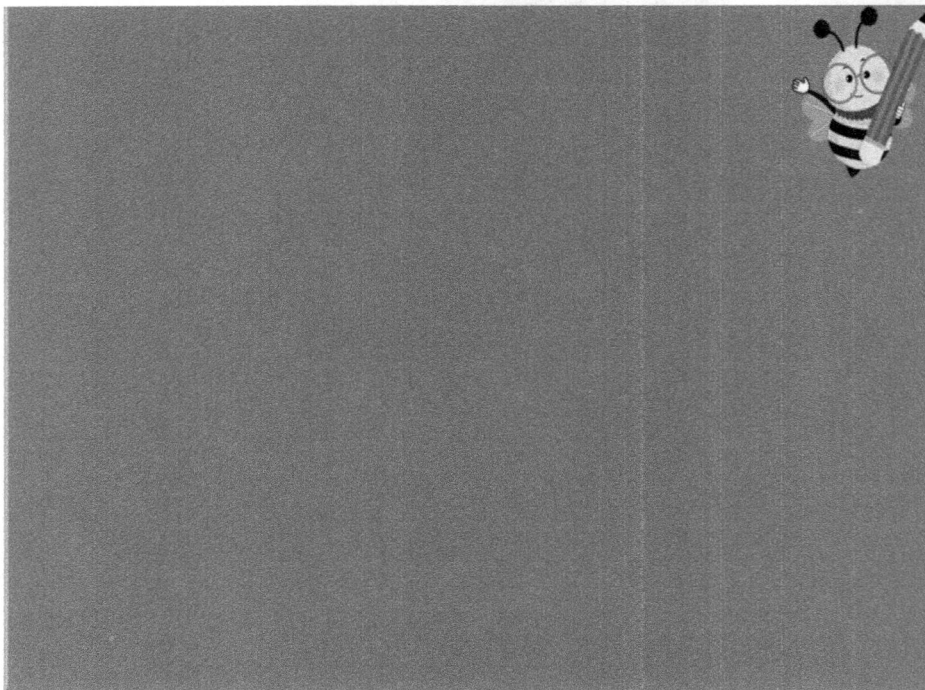

Pancake Method Table:

1-Bedroom Apartment	
Groceries	
Restaurants	
Health Insurance	
Public Transport	
Internet	
Phone	
Heating / AC	
Other Expenses:	
Visa	
Round Trip Air Ticket once a year	
Total	

Explore Exciting Jobs and their Salaries.

So, you're wondering what to do with your life? What major do you want to choose for college? What are you interested in? Do you want to be an artist? An Engineer?

Before you start working on your choices, knowledge is important. We suggest you talk to professionals in your area of interest to see what it's like working in the field.

We'd also like you to complete the two activities below so you have an idea of how much you would earn for different professions as well. We aren't saying that you should always go for the highest paid job. But knowledge is key, and you should at least be aware of what different jobs are paid.

Match these professions with their average annual salaries in 2023.

Lifeguards	$26060
Hotel Clerk	$33190
Recreation Attendants	$29010
Engineer	$27330
Shampooers	$100261
Anaesthesiologist	$311460
Maids	$26110
Neurologist	$28040
Fast Food Workers	$276660
Waiter	$25160
Programmer	$167160
Dentist	$91441
Cafeteria Attendants	$29580
Oral Surgeon	$27690

Organize these jobs in the order of increasing salary:

Childcare Workers

Cardiologist

Cooks

Cashiers

Computer and Information Systems Manager

Dermatologist

Airline Pilot

Hotel Hosts

Paediatric Surgeon

Gambling dealers

Stock Market Time: Ride This Exciting Wave

Now, it's time for the topic you've been waiting for. Welcome to the fun world of the stock market, where you own a slice of your dreams.

Think of your favorite companies. The ones that make video games like Sony, or the ones that sell ice creams like Baskins and Robbins. All these companies are each composed of several pieces of ownership, called shares. These shares are traded on a marketplace called the stock market. In the marketplace you can buy or sell 1 or more shares of a particular company.

So, who are the major players? The people who buy stocks of a company are known as the investors in a company. They study, analyse and decide which stocks they want to buy.

To make sure everything is fair and square, there are referees called "brokers." They help investors buy and sell stocks, keep track of all the transactions, and make sure everyone plays by the rules. Without them, it would be chaos! These days, a lot of brokerages are online, and all the trades are conducted over the internet.

So, how does this work? Let's look at an example. Company A is worth $100. It decides to issue 20 shares. So, each share is worth $5 ($100 divided by 20). Bob buys 2 shares. So, Bob spends $10 to buy 2 shares.

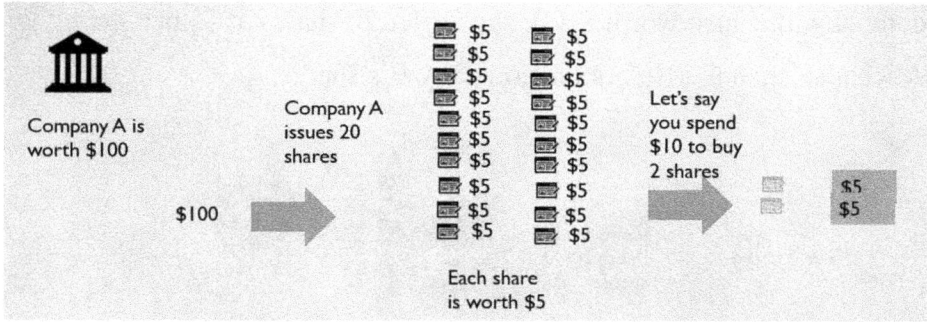

Company A is worth $100

$100 → Company A issues 20 shares

$5 $5
$5 $5
$5 $5
$5 $5
$5 $5
$5 $5
$5 $5
$5 $5
$5 $5
$5 $5

Each share is worth $5

Let's say you spend $10 to buy 2 shares →

$5
$5

So, now let's look at this 10 years later. The stocks are now worth $25 each. So, Bob's 2 shares are now worth $50. So, if Bob decides to sell his shares now, he made **$40** ($50-$10).

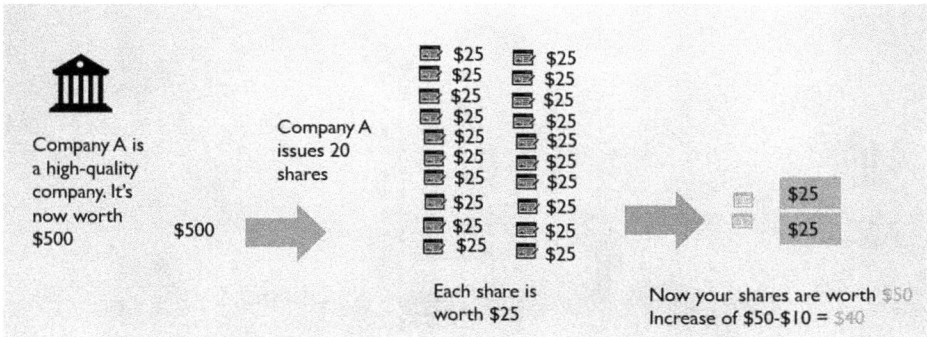

Company A is a high-quality company. It's now worth $500

$500 → Company A issues 20 shares

$25 $25
$25 $25
$25 $25
$25 $25
$25 $25
$25 $25
$25 $25
$25 $25
$25 $25
$25 $25

Each share is worth $25

→

$25
$25

Now your shares are worth $50
Increase of $50-$10 = $40

But remember shares can also go down in price. Now, let's look at Alice who invested in 2 shares of company B. Company B is a low-quality company. It is also worth $100, and issues 20 shares at $5 per share. Alice also spends $10, but on Company B's shares.

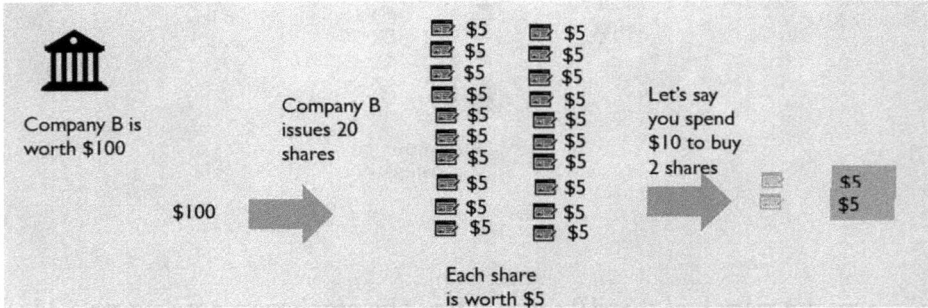

Company B is worth $100 · $100 → Company B issues 20 shares · Each share is worth $5 · Let's say you spend $10 to buy 2 shares → $5 $5

After 10 years, however, the stock goes down in price to $8 per share. So, Alice loses $2 per share, or $4 in total.

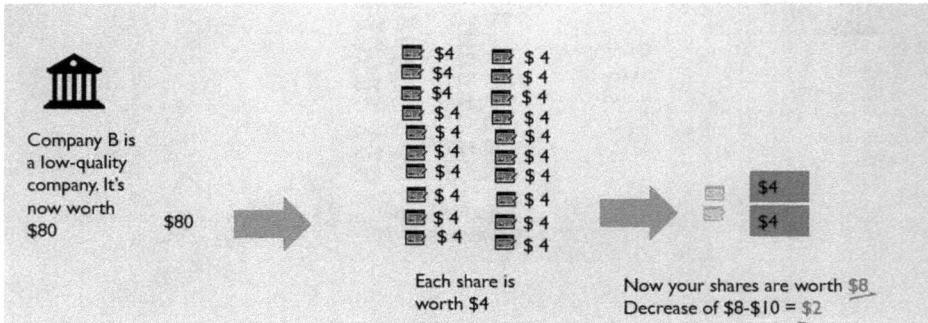

Company B is a low-quality company. It's now worth $80 · $80 → Each share is worth $4 → Now your shares are worth $8. Decrease of $8-$10 = $2

So, the quality of the company is essential when deciding which one to invest in.

Stock Market Dividends

As you just learnt, you can make money from a stock when it goes up in price. But some companies also pay you to own the stock. This is known as a dividend payment. A dividend payment is a portion of the stock's profits distributed to shareholders.

So, let's look at a company C. It pays a 10% dividend annually. It is also valued at $100, with 20 shares at $5. Tim decides to buy 2 shares of the company. He spends $10.

Regardless of whether the stocks go up or down, he gets paid a 10% dividend on his investment. He gets paid $1 a year (10% of $10) for the period of time he holds the stock.

You got 10 shares of Apple at $100 a share. It has a dividend of 2% per year. If you sell after 2 years at $150 per share, how much money did you make?

   i.   Calculate the dividend.

  ii.   Increase in value of investment.

You got 15 shares of Intel at $50 a share. It has a dividend of 5% per year. If you sell after 1 year at $125 per share, how much money did you make?

i.   Calculate the dividend.

ii.   Increase in value of investment.

iii.   Total Profit

So, here's the most important question. How do you choose what stock to invest in? What's a good stock? Or a bad stock? Analysing a stock is beyond the scope of this book, and I actually recommend the book Security Analysis for anyone who's interested.

In this section, however, I want you to understand the concept of risk and return. Whenever you invest in something, you have to understand the risk you are taking. Nothing is free of risk. You might think that keeping cash in the bank is risk free. However, the bank can go bankrupt. You might also think that keeping your money in a safe at home is risk free. However, you could get robbed; and also the money loses value over time with inflation.

So, what's a risky investment? What's a safe investment? It's all relative. Investing in a penny stock is riskier than investing in Apple stock. And Apple stock may be riskier than an index fund. And, generally the higher the risk the higher the possible returns. Also, the higher the risk, the lower the probability of that return. For example, if you invest in a penny stock, there's a much higher return possible. However, the chances of getting that return are very small, and most likely you will lose all the money invested in the penny stock.

Here's a flow of investments with risk and reward.

The investments at the bottom have the highest risk and the ones at the top have the lowest risk.

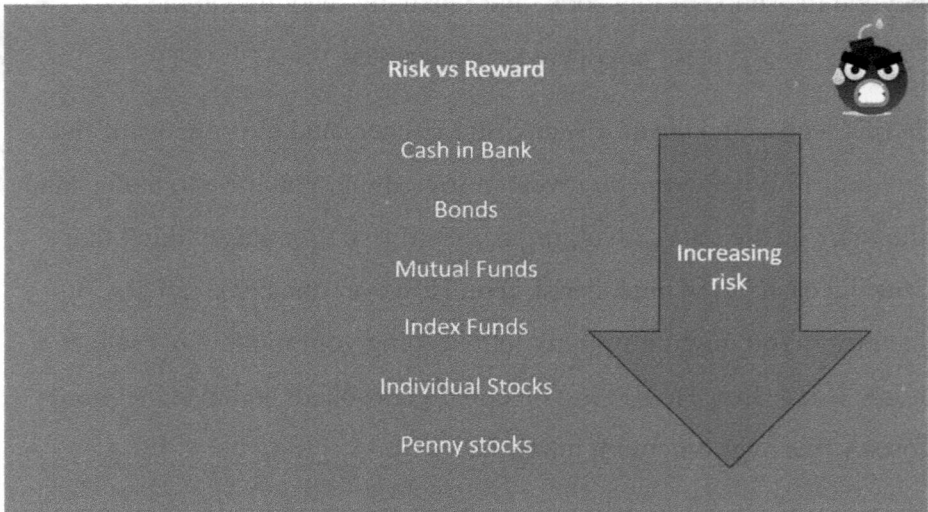

You might have heard about Bonds in the stock market. Bonds are an essential park of the stock market and the economy. But very few people know what they are. Even fewer know exactly how they work.

A Bond is basically a loan with a fixed interest rate. If you invest in a bond, you are loaning someone money for a certain period of time. At the end of the period, you get your entire money back. You also get paid a fixed amount of money at regular intervals.

For example, let's say that cool video game company in your city wants to expand its operations. It needs $10000 and decides to issue a $10000 bond at 6% annual interest rate for 5 years.

Sam is interested in investing in the bond. Sam invests $10000 in the bond. That means he gets $10000 back after 5 years.

He also gets an amount every year with an interest rate of 6%.

Interest that Sam receives $= 6\%$ of $\$10000 = \frac{6}{100} X10000 = \$600$

So, Sam gets $600 every year. This 6% or $600 is called the **coupon payment**. $10000 is the **face value** of the bond. 5 years is the **maturity period** of the bond. The diagram below explains Sam's investment clearly.

84

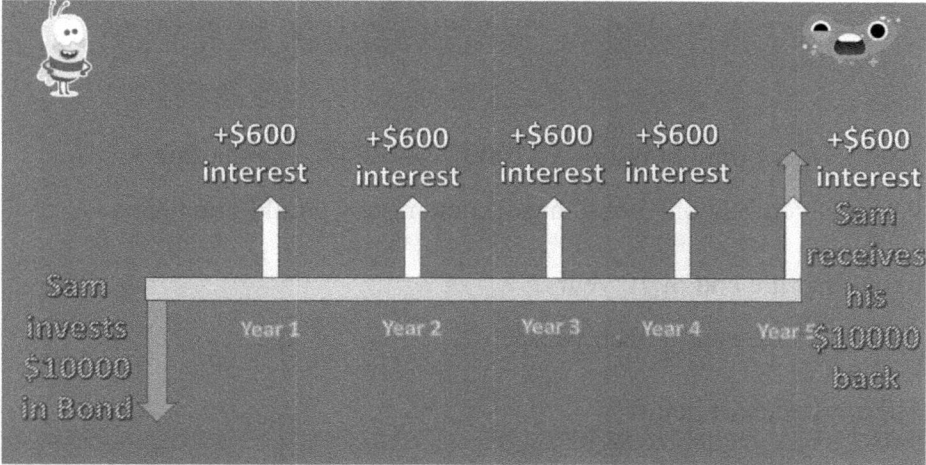

Now, it's time for you to work on an example.

The US Government issues a $1000 bond at 4% interest rate for 10 years. If you buy one bond, how much money would you receive:

    a.   At the end of 10 years?

    b.   At the end of each year?

Fill out the chart below:

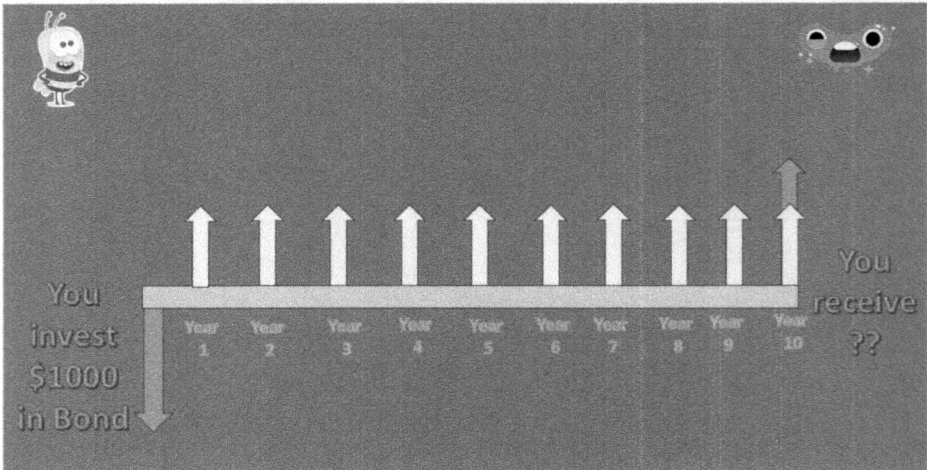

The Bond Marketplace

Did you know that there is also a marketplace for bonds where you can sell your bonds before the maturity period. In the previous video game example, let's say Sam buys the $10000 bond for a maturity period of 5 years. After 2 years, the video game manufacturer offers a 5-year bond at only 3% interest rates. That interest rate is very low compared to the bond that Sam owns. The bond Sam owns suddenly becomes valued higher as it pays a higher interest rate. Sam's bond is now valued at $12000. So, Sam has the option to now:

A. Hold the bond to maturity and get $600 interest every year as in previous example.

B. Sell the bond in the bond marketplace for $12000 now and forego the interest payments.

So, you can make money on bonds in the marketplace as well as with the interest payments.

Let's look at Option B, where Sam sells the bond in the marketplace for $12000.

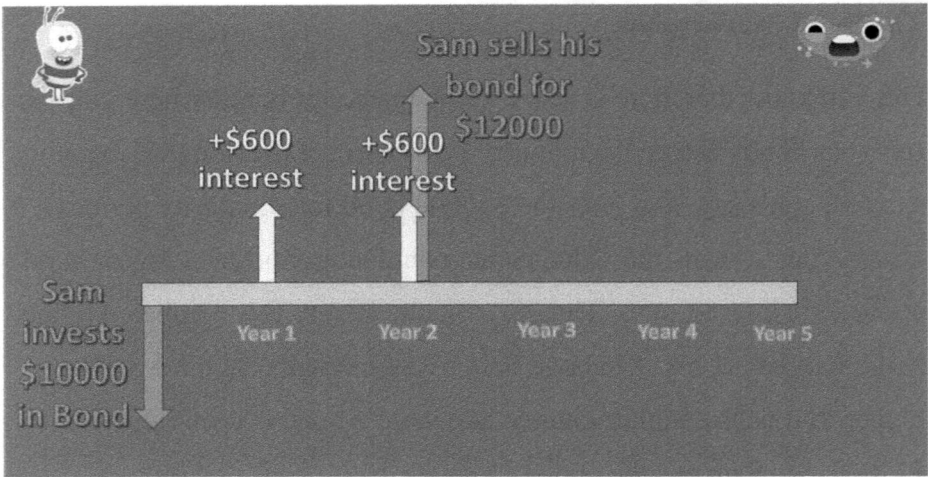

Sam sells his bond for $12000

+$600 interest   +$600 interest

Sam invests $10000 in Bond

Year 1   Year 2   Year 3   Year 4   Year 5

So, Sam makes a profit of $2000 in addition to the $1200 he receives in interest for the first two years.

Of course, keep in mind that if the video game company offers a bond after 2 years at a higher interest rate (let's say 10%), then the value of Sam's bond goes down. If this happens, Sam can just pick Option A and receive $600 interest every year plus the face value at the end of 5 years.

Challenge 26

So, let's work on another example. Let's say, the US Government issues a $1000 bond at 4% interest rate for 10 years. You invest in 1 bond. After 3 years, the US Government offers another 10-year bond for 6%. Does the value of your bond go up or down?

Challenge 27

In the previous problem, the US Government offers another 10-year bond for 2%. Does the value of your bond go up or down?

Apple offers a 6-year $1000 bond for 6% annual interest. Both Adam and Bobby invest in the bond. Adam holds the bond to maturity, while Bobby holds it for 3 years. At the end of 3 years, Bobby notices that Apple is offering the 6-year bond for only 3% interest. So, the value of his bond went to $1200. Bobby sells his bond in the open market.

How much do Bobby and Adam make on their initial $1000 investment? Work it out below.

Are you ready to take the next step and start your journey? Before you start doing so, make sure you understand the concepts in this book. Work out these questions in the quiz below that's based on the information in this book.

If you're struggling to do so, visit the chapter relevant to the question.

If you still have a question that just does not make sense, make sure to email me at abiprod.pty.ltd@gmail.com

1. Andy invests \$600 in a mutual fund with an annual compound interest rate of 4%. How much Andy have after 7 years?

2. Jiten puts $2000 into a savings account with a compound interest rate of 4.5%. How much Jiten have after 8 years?

3. Sinner takes out a loan of $10,000 with a compound interest rate of 3%. He decides to start paying the loan back after 5 years. How much will Sinner owe after 5 years?

4. Mary invests $1500 in a fixed deposit account with a compound interest rate of 8% annually. How much does Mary have after 5 years?

5. Edward puts $3000 in a retirement account with a compound interest rate of 9.2%. How much money Edward have after 20 years?

6. In 2020, the price of a new smartphone is $800. If the rate of inflation is 4.1% per year, what will be the cost of the same smartphone in 2026?

7. A family's monthly grocery expenses amount to $500 in 2022. Assuming an annual inflation rate of 4.8%, what will be their expected monthly grocery bill in 2030?

8. The rent for an apartment is currently $1200 per month in 2023. The rate of inflation averages 6% per year. What will the apartment rent for in 2030?

9. A company's annual subscription fee for its software product is $250 in 2021. The inflation rate is 4.2% per year on average. What will be the expected cost of the subscription in 2028?

10. Jacob currently lives in New York City and is thinking about relocating to Los Angeles next month. He spends $4,500 a month in New York. Use the pancake method to estimate how much he would be expected to spend in Los Angeles if he decides to move there. Show your calculations below.

11. Steven is thinking about moving from Atlanta to Houston. His current monthly expenses in Atlanta are $3800. How much is she expected to spend monthly in Houston? Use the pancake method to estimate her costs.

12. Bob purchased 25 shares of Verizon at $30 per share. The stock pays an annual dividend of 7%. After holding the shares for 3 years, Bob decides to sell them at $40 per share.

Calculate:

i.   The total dividend earned over 3 years.

ii.   The increase in the value of Bob's investment.

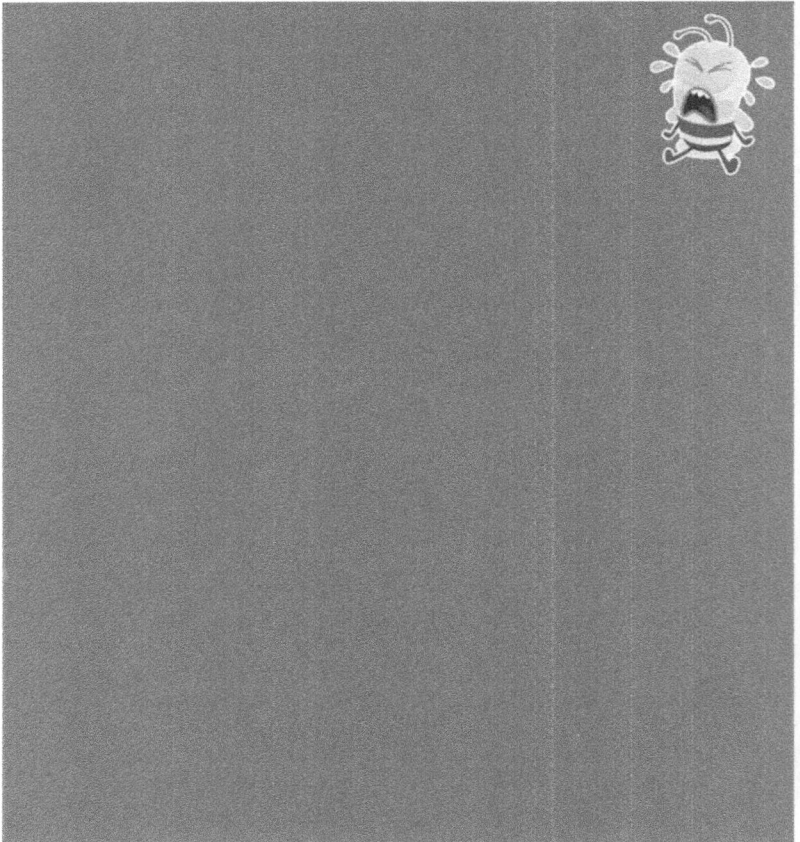

13. Alice invests in 20 shares of Microsoft at $240 per share. The stock offers a dividend of 1.8% annually. After holding the shares for 4 years, Alice decides to sell them at $360 per share. Calculate:

    i.   The total dividend received during the 4-year period.

    ii.   The increase in the value of Alice's investment.

14. Mary buys 12 shares of Amazon at $100 per share. The stock pays no dividend. After holding the shares for 5 years, Mary decides to sell them at $150 per share.

Calculate:

i.   The total dividend received over 5 years.

ii.   The increase in the value of Mary's investment.

15. Jim acquires 25 shares of Facebook at $150 per share. The stock has no dividend. After holding the shares for 2 years, Jim sells them at $300 per share.

Calculate:

i.   The total dividend earned over the 2-year period.

ii.   The increase in the value of Jim's investment.

16. Carl invests in 8 shares of United Health at $400 per share. The stock offers a dividend of 2% per year. After holding the shares for 6 years, Carl sells them at $900 per share.

Calculate:

i. The total dividend received during the 6-year period.

ii. The increase in the value of Carl's investment.

17. The US Government offers a 5-year bond with a 3% annual interest rate. You invest $5000 in this bond. After holding it for 3 years, the government announces a new 5-year bond with a 4% interest rate. Does the value of your bond go up or down?

18. Company XYZ issues a 7-year $2000 bond with a 5% annual interest rate. Two investors, Alice and Bob, buy the bond at the same time. Alice holds the bond to maturity, while Bob sells it after 4 years. At the end of 4 years, the market interest rate for a 7-year bond of similar risk drops to 3%, and the value of the bond goes up to $3000. If Bob sells his bond in the open market, how much does he make on his initial $2000 investment? How much does Alice make on her investment when the bond matures?

19. Tech Inc. offers a 10-year $5000 bond with an 8% annual interest rate. Both Emily and James invest in the bond. Emily holds the bond to maturity, while James sells it after 6 years. At the end of 6 years, Tech Inc. announces a new 10-year bond with a 6% interest rate. So, the value of James's bond increases to $5500. James decides to sell his bond in the open market. Calculate how much Emily and James make on their initial $5000 investment.

20. The City Municipality issues a 15-year $10,000 bond with a 4% annual interest rate. You invest in this bond. After holding it for 8 years, you notice that the market interest rate for a 15-year bond of similar risk has risen to 6%. Does the value of your bond go up or down?

Answers

```
D N E G Q G Y Z H S B L P K U
X U M V U M T Y N K O V L Q W
I H O E V U F H A O D J V C Z
N L V J I S E V N I H N J R D
V U R D Y S A V I N G S B Z L
I I D E A M J X F Q H I Z Z V
K F N E R P R O F I T G E A A
W O U G X X B P Z N J V O S G
M I F E Y V S Q V E Y Y M E F
B Q J Z P F T A E E U X Q J Z
U T I Y L M K N A B R I K O O
H F Q L Z L M M W A E A E F K
N H S H R X E V D G R J H S E
R M A S L P W S I D T Y R S U
D D C U R R E N C Y F S S R M
```

Challenge 2

```
N V G U Z H T W O R G G P A K
I E N Y E F J L U C P X B K U
A N C I N J Q W C X A S D P E
L H T N W A A P E T O S T I F
V K A E A K P Y E N Q M E U D
T D E Z R W H M X U J Q G Y C
G S I B U E O W O O K G D X A
O N Q V U N S L O C M R U H E
X Q O X I T H T L C B B B S N
B T V G O D S E U A G S Y X X
M F L C V F E F I K M W K G Q
B O K A X Q T N R N S L B F T
U C L B H E L F D A W I O A S
N U V S I X Y I A B Y Y R L U
E Y F U Q A V M J I O B S H L
```

Challenge 3

```
B O B N N V C T X F M W I G C
Y V N F O B A I Z A W H M M H
N L H H K I N P R X Y D J P W
Y U R I G H T K Y L E A G G W
X L L U C D E A U E Q C P D Z
K R M W E T M U L D A H Y T A
Z R J K Z N T M O F A A L L H
S H E M B C E A J P N R X N A
G M Z E V R F R M T K I H X T
W O R O P E N E P X I T I V E
X A E M C A P T O E E Y J Q G
O R T A A Q G P X B R D O N D
I N C O M E N C K L C T O Y U
F I N A N C E K L Z N O N B B
B W B U D G E T I N G X Z E G
```

Challenge 4

```
O K A I H D S I Q Z A R I M O
Y E M L Q G D R R M L V N W Y
D N O B P I Y I I B Q N V H V
N D R P B H B X N J A I E D T
N U K V S N S C S T E J S M O
H I Q V W M X D W V E P T V C
N V B V O X M N N J G R M F G
Z W N Y N L F U C H G W E A I
Y U O U U V S F P O W Y N S K
N Z B T Q U U L I M F S T E T
O D C C P P M A L D S Y W B M
K I N D E X F U N D T B E D M
K J X G R Q J T X M O P G A G
D O X O O R X U V V C N I I N
T X S H A J F M R U K K A M W
```

116

Challenge 5

			¹m						²c		
³p	r	o	f	⁴i	t				u		
			o		n				⁵r	i	s	k
⁶s	h	a	r	e		n			r		
e			y		v			e		
l				⁷s	a	v	i	n	g	
l				t			c		
			⁸b	u	y	
			a		
			n		
			k		

Challenge 6

		¹b			²e
		u			n
		d			t
		g			r
		e			e
³f	t			p
i	i			r
n	n			e
⁴s	a	v	i	n	g	s	a	c	c	o	u	n	t
n.				e
⁵s	t	o	c	k		⁶v	a	l	u	e
i				r
⁷c	o	m	p	a	n	y
l
g
⁸a	l	l	o	w	a	n	c	e
a
l

117

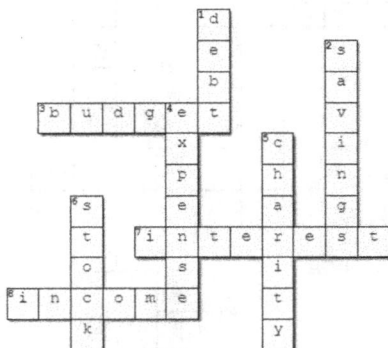

Challenge 13

$$A = 1000\left(1 + \frac{7}{100}\right)^{10} = \$1967.15$$

Challenge 14

	Amount Added	Interest	Total after interest + savings
End of Year 1	$1000		$1000
End of Year 2	$1000	$1000*1.05=$1050	$2050
End of Year 3	$1000	$2050*1.05=$2152.5	$3152.5
End of Year 4	$1000	$3310.13	**$4310.13**

So, Andy has $4310.13 at the end of 4 years.

$$NP = 30\left(1 + \frac{4}{100}\right)^{10} = \$44.41$$

$$NP = 300\left(1 + \frac{5}{100}\right)^{10} = \$488.66$$

Ally is richer as the $100 is worth more in 1970. $100 is worth a lot less in 2020 due to inflation.

$$NP = 100\left(1 + \frac{100}{100}\right)^{6} = 6400\ Bolivars$$

Challenge 19

NUMBEO

Select City

Cost Of Living ▾ Property Prices ▾ Quality Of Life ▾ Premium ▾

Cost of Living › Compare Cities › United States vs United States › San Francisco, CA vs Miami, FL

Cost of Living Comparison Between San Francisco, CA and Miami, FL ⇆

You would need around 7,395.2$ in Miami, FL to maintain the same standard of life that you can have with 9,100.0$ in San Francisco, CA (assuming you rent in both cities). This calculation uses our Cost of Living Plus Rent Index to compare the cost of living and assume net earnings (after income tax). You can change the amount in this calculation.

Indices Difference

Consumer Prices in Miami, FL are 15.7% lower than in San Francisco, CA (without rent)
Consumer Prices Including Rent in Miami, FL are 18.7% lower than in San Francisco, CA
Rent Prices in Miami, FL are 22.3% lower than in San Francisco, CA
Restaurant Prices in Miami, FL are 2.4% lower than in San Francisco, CA
Groceries Prices in Miami, FL are 18.8% lower than in San Francisco, CA
Local Purchasing Power in Miami, FL is 14.4% lower than in San Francisco, CA

Cost of living in Miami using Pancake Method = $6000*0.83 = **$4980**

Shampooers → $25160

Fast Food Workers → $26060

Recreation Attendants →$26110

Lifeguards → $27330

Cafeteria Attendants → $27690

Hotel Clerks → $28040

Waiters → $29010

Maids → $29580

Anaesthesiologists → $33190

Oral Surgeons → $311460

Neurologists → $276660

Dentists → $167160

Engineers → $100261

Programmers → $91441

Cooks → $25490

Hosts → $26000.

Cashiers → $26770

Childcare Workers → $27680

Gambling dealers → $28960

Cardiologist → $353970

Dermatologist → $302740

Paediatric Surgeon → $290310

Airline Pilot → $198190

Computer and Information Systems Manager → $162930

Challenge 23

i.   Cost of shares = 10 x $100 = $1000

Dividend = 2% of $1000 = $20 per year

Dividend for 2 years = $20 x 2 = **$40 for two years**

ii.   Original cost of shares = $1000

Sales price of shares = 10 x $150 = $1500

Profit = $1500 - $1000 = **$500**

Challenge 24

i.   Cost of shares = 15 x $50 = $750

Dividend = 5% of $750 = **$37.5 per year**

ii.   Original cost of shares = $750

Sales price of shares = 15 x $125 = $1875

Profit = $1875 - $750 = **$1125**

iii.   Total Profit with Dividend = $1125 + $37.5 = **$1162.5**

Interest = 4% x $1000 = $40 per year

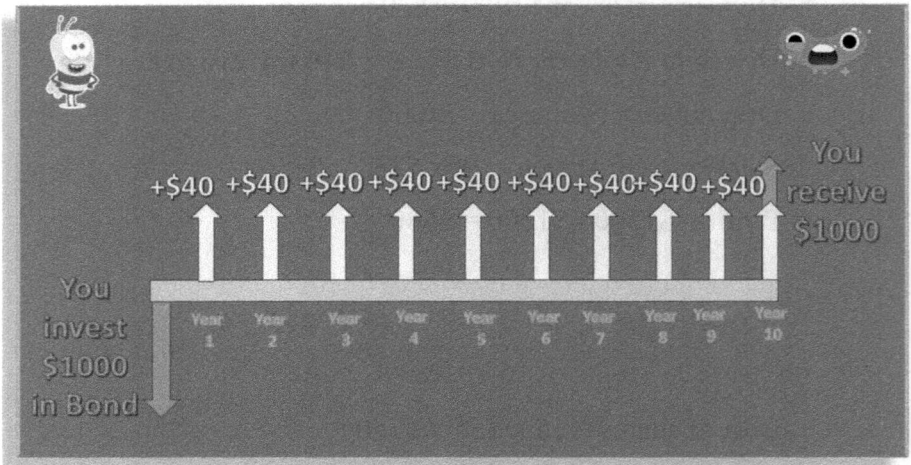

a. You receive the bond face value of $1000 back after 10 years

b. You receive an annual interest of $40

The value of the bond goes down.

The value of the bond goes up.

Bobby:

Interest = 6% of $1000 = $60 per year for 3 years

Total Interest = $60 x 3 years = $180

Increase in value of bond = $1200 - $1000 = $200

Total Profit for Bobby = $200 + $180 = **$380**

Adam:

Interest = 6% of $1000 = $60 per year for 3 years

Total Interest = $60 x 5 years = $300

No change in value of bond for Adam as he holds it to maturity

Total Profit for Adam = **$300**

So Bobby makes $380 while Adam makes $300.

The Ultimate Savings Challenge

1. $789.56

2. $2844.2

3. $11,592.74

4. $2040.73

5. $17441.11

6. $1018.11

7. $727.55

8. $1804.36

9. $332.43

10. $3852

11. $3442.8

12.

i. $157.5

ii. $250

13.

i. $345.6

ii. $2400

14.

iii. $0

iv. $600

15.

i. $0

ii. $3750

16.

i. $384

ii. $4000

17. Bond Value Goes Down

18. Bond Value Goes Down

19. Bob makes $1400. Alice Makes $700.

20. Emily makes $4000, while James $2900

21. The bond value goes down.

Appendix

Data for Chapter "Explore Exciting Jobs and Their Salaries"

https://www.thebalancemoney.com/top-worst-paid-jobs-2061699

https://www.investopedia.com/personal-finance/top-highest-paying-jobs/